Made in the USA
Monee, IL
15 January 2021

57696232R00066